The White House ABC

A Presidential Alphabet

PRESIDENT GEORGE WASHINGTON

THE WHITE HOUSE ABC

A PRESIDENTIAL ALPHABET

John Hutton

White House Historical Association

2003

White House Historical Association

The White House Historical Association is a nonprofit organization, chartered on November 3, 1961, to enhance understanding, appreciation, and enjoyment of the historic White House. Income from the sale of the association's books and guides is returned to the publications program and is used as well to acquire historical furnishings and memorabilia for the White House. For more information, address inquiries to www.whitehousehistory.org.

Chairman: Henry A. Dudley Jr.
President: Neil W. Horstman
Director of Publications: Marcia Mallet Anderson
Publications Specialist: Doyle S. Rice
Editorial Consultant: Ann Hofstra Grogg
Other WHHA Staff Contributors: William B. Bushong, Constance McCulloch, Vanessa York Piccorossi, Sharon Pierce, John Riley
Office of the Curator, The White House, Staff Contributors: Curator: William G. Allman; Assistant Curator: Lydia Tederick; Curator Emeritus: Betty C. Monkman

Translators
Latin—W. Marshall Johnston Jr. and Pamela D. Lackie
French, Spanish, German—Bowne Global Solutions

Design and Typography
Thornwillow Press, Ltd.

Drawings Copyright © 2004 John Hutton
Compilation Copyright © 2004 White House Historical Association

ISBN 0-912308-88-5

FIRST EDITION
10 9 8 7 6 5 4 3 2 1
Printed in Canada

For my parents . . .

PICTURES OLD AND NEW

This volume brings together people and things from throughout the history of the White House. We are accustomed to the idea that modern people work in this venerable historical setting. But what if past residents were able to time-travel and find themselves in today's White House—their former home? Why not imagine what would happen if old and new rooms, objects, furniture, presidents, first families, and famous visitors could meet and mix, alphabetically, in the pages of our little book?

Readers are advised that the word lists for each letter of the alphabet are presented in five languages: English, French, German, Spanish, and Latin. Translations of the presidents' first names are provided where practicable and appropriate.

This book is intended both to amuse and to teach. Many hundreds of historical details wait to be discovered in the drawings—from portraits of presidents, first families, and famous visitors, to displays of beautiful furniture and other decorative arts, to views of the interior and exterior of the White House itself. We hope as you "visit" these pages, using the Historical Notes at the end as your guide, that you will gain a deeper appreciation for the White House, its remarkable treasures, and its fascinating history.

The author is deeply indebted to the staff of the White House Historical Association for their help. Special thanks are due to Betty C. Monkman, Curator Emeritus, the White House.

A

·ABCDEFGHIJKLMNOPQRSTUVWXYZ

a

John Adams	*Jean Adams*	*Johann Adams*	*Juan Adams*	*Ioannes Adami*
John Quincy Adams	*Jean Quincy Adams*	*Johann Quincy Adams*	*Juan Quincy Adams*	*Ioannes Quintus Adami*
Chester A. Arthur	*Chester A. Arthur*	*Chester A. Arthur*	*Chester A. Arthur*	*Castrensis Artorius*
Architect	*Architecte*	*Architekt*	*Arquitecto*	*Architectus*
Artisan	*Artisan*	*Künstler*	*Artesano*	*Artifex*
Arrival	*Arrivée*	*Ankunft*	*Llegada*	*Adventus*
Auspicious!	*Prometteur!*	*Vielverheissend!*	*¡Oportuna!*	*Fausta!*

PRESIDENT CHESTER A. ARTHUR

PRESIDENT JOHN QUINCY ADAMS

FIRST LADY ABIGAIL ADAMS

JAMES HOBAN   PRESIDENT JOHN ADAMS

B
b

A · C D E F G H I J K L M N O P Q R S T U V W X Y Z

James Buchanan	*Jacques Buchanan*	*Jakob Buchanan*	*Jaime Buchanan*	*Iacobus Bucananus*
George Bush	*Georges Bush*	*Georg Bush*	*Jorge Bush*	*Georgius Myrtus*
George W. Bush	*Georges W. Bush*	*Georg W. Bush*	*Jorge W. Bush*	*Georgius Ambulator Myrtus*
Blue Room	*Salon Bleu*	*Das blaue Zimmer*	*Salón Azul*	*Caeruleum Conclave*
Beautiful building!	*Belle demeure!*	*Herrliches gebäude!*	*¡Hermoso edificio!*	*Pulchrum aedificium!*

JAPANESE DELEGATION TO PRESIDENT BUCHANAN'S WHITE HOUSE, 1860

PRESIDENT GEORGE W. BUSH

PRESIDENT GEORGE BUSH

PRESIDENT JAMES BUCHANAN

Grover Cleveland	*Grover Cleveland*	*Grover Cleveland*	*Grover Cleveland*	*Nemorarius Clivosa*
Calvin Coolidge	*Calvin Coolidge*	*Calvin Coolidge*	*Calvino Coolidge*	*Calvinus Frigidus*
Jimmy Carter	*Jimmy Carter*	*Jimmy Carter*	*Jimmy Carter*	*Iacobus Mulio*
William J. Clinton	*Guillaume J. Clinton*	*Wilhelm J. Clinton*	*Guillermo J. Clinton*	*Gulielmus Altoppidum*
China Room	*Salon de Porcelaine*	*Porzellanzimmer*	*Salón de la Porcelana*	*Cella cubiculum*
Cat	*Chat*	*Katze*	*Gato*	*Feles*
Curious!	*Curieux!*	*Neugierig!*	*¡Curioso!*	*Curiosa!*

PRESIDENT WILLIAM J. CLINTON   PRESIDENT CALVIN COOLIDGE

PRESIDENT JIMMY CARTER   PRESIDENT GROVER CLEVELAND

The China Room

Dance	*Danse*	*Tanz*	*Baile*	*Saltatio*
Dazzling	*Éblouissant*	*Blendend*	*Deslumbrantes*	*Nitens*
Dresses	*Robes*	*Kleider*	*Vestidos*	*Stolae*
Dog	*Chien*	*Hund*	*Perro*	*Canis*
Delightful!	*Amusant!*	*Reizend!*	*¡Encantador!*	*Dulcis!*

FREDERICK DOUGLASS

Dancing in the East Room

Dwight D. Eisenhower	*Dwight D. Eisenhower*	*Dwight D. Eisenhower*	*Dwight D. Eisenhower*	*Dionysius Ferreadolabra*
Easter Egg Roll	*Course aux oeufs de Pâques*	*Ostereier-Rollspiel*	*Carrera con Huevos de Pascua*	*Paschalium Ovorum Gyrus*
Eagle	*Aigle*	*Adler*	*Águila*	*Aquila*
Executive Mansion	*Résidence Présidentielle*	*Wohnsitz des Präsidenten*	*Mansión Ejecutiva*	*Domus Consularis*
Enjoyable!	*Amusant!*	*Unterhaltsam!*	*¡Agradable!*	*Iucundus!*

President Dwight D. Eisenhower

Millard Fillmore	*Millard Fillmore*	*Millard Fillmore*	*Millard Fillmore*	*Millardus Completior*
Gerald R. Ford	*Géralde R. Ford*	*Gerold R. Ford*	*Geraldo R. Ford*	*Geraldus Vadum*
Flying	*Voler*	*Wehen*	*Ondea*	*Volans*
Flag	*Drapeau*	*Fahne*	*Bandera*	*Vexillum*
Freedom!	*Liberté!*	*Freiheit!*	*¡Libertad!*	*Libertas!*

FIRST LADY LAURA BUSH

PRESIDENT MILLARD FILLMORE   PRESIDENT GERALD R. FORD

Ulysses S. Grant	*Ulysse S. Grant*	*Ulysses S. Grant*	*Ulises S. Grant*	*Ulysses Concessio*
James A. Garfield	*Jacques A. Garfield*	*Jakob A. Garfield*	*Jaime A. Garfield*	*Iacobus Piscager*
Garden	*Jardin*	*Garten*	*Jardín*	*Hortus*
Gate	*Portail*	*Tor*	*Puerta*	*Porta*
Geranium	*Géranium*	*Geranie*	*Geranio*	*Geranium*
General!	*Général!*	*General!*	*¡General!*	*Imperator!*

PRESIDENT JAMES A. GARFIELD   PRESIDENT ULYSSES S. GRANT

H
A B C D E F G · I J K L M N O P Q R S T U V W X Y Z
h

William Henry Harrison	*Guillaume H. Harrison*	*Wilhelm H. Harrison*	*Guillermo H. Harrison*	*Gulielmus Henrici*
Rutherford B. Hayes	*Rutherford B. Hayes*	*Rutherford B. Hayes*	*Rutherford B. Hayes*	*Ruterfordus Faena*
Benjamin Harrison	*Benjamin Harrison*	*Benjamin Harrison*	*Benjamin Harrison*	*Benjaminus Henrici*
Warren G. Harding	*Warren G. Harding*	*Warren G. Harding*	*Warren G. Harding*	*Saeptum Fortis*
Herbert Hoover	*Herbert Hoover*	*Herbert Hoover*	*Heriberto Hoover*	*Herbertus Hoverius*
North Entrance Hall	*Hall d'entrée Nord*	*Eingangshalle*	*Vestíbulo de la Entrada Norte*	*Atrium Septentrionale*
Horse	*Cheval*	*Pferd*	*Caballo*	*Equus*
Handshake	*Poignée de main*	*Handschlag*	*Apretón de manos*	*Dextrum Dare*
Hail to the Chief!	*Salut au Chef!*	*Hoch lebe unser Oberhaupt!*	*¡Saluden al Jefe!*	*Ave Princeps!*

PRESIDENT WILLIAM HENRY HARRISON *(on horseback)*

PRESIDENT RUTHERFORD B. HAYES   PRESIDENT HERBERT HOOVER

PRESIDENT BENJAMIN HARRISON   PRESIDENT WARREN G. HARDING

Inauguration	*Investiture*	*Einweihung*	*Inauguración*	*Consecratio*
Impressive	*Impressionnant*	*Eindrucksvoll*	*Impresionante*	*Splendida*
Important	*Important*	*Wichtig*	*Importante*	*Gravis*
I do solemnly swear!	*Je jure solennellement!*	*Das will ich feierlich schwören!*	*"¡Juro solemnemente!"*	*Solemne Iuro!*

CHIEF JUSTICE EARL WARREN
PRESIDENT DWIGHT D. EISENHOWER

PRESIDENT RONALD REAGAN
CHIEF JUSTICE WARREN BURGER

PRESIDENT RUTHERFORD B. HAYES
CHIEF JUSTICE MORRISON WAITE

J
j

A B C D E F G H I · K L M N O P Q R S T U V W X Y Z

Thomas Jefferson	*Thomas Jefferson*	*Thomas Jefferson*	*Tomás Jefferson*	*Geminus Godafridi*
Andrew Jackson	*Andrew Jackson*	*André Jackson*	*Andreu Jackson*	*Andréas Ioannis*
Andrew Johnson	*Andrew Johnson*	*André Johnson*	*Andreu Johnson*	*Andréas Ioannis*
Lyndon B. Johnson	*Lyndon B. Johnson*	*Lyndon B. Johnson*	*Lyndon B. Johnson*	*Arbormons Ioannis*
Journey	*Voyage*	*Reise*	*Viaje*	*Iter*
Journal	*Journal*	*Journal*	*Diario*	*Acta Diurna*
Joyful!	*Joyeux!*	*Voller Freude!*	*¡Alegre!*	*Laetus!*

PRESIDENT ANDREW JOHNSON

PRESIDENT LYNDON B. JOHNSON

PRESIDENT ANDREW JACKSON

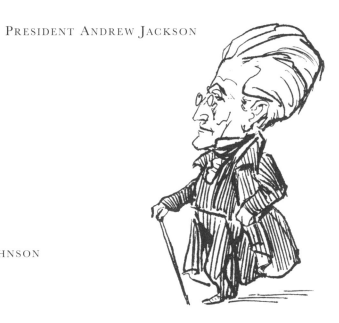

WILLIAM CLARK   MERIWETHER LEWIS

SACAJAWEA

PRESIDENT THOMAS JEFFERSON

K

A B C D E F G H I J · L M N O P Q R S T U V W X Y Z

k

John F. Kennedy	*Jean F. Kennedy*	*Johann F. Kennedy*	*Juan F. Kennedy*	*Ioannes Informicaput*
Jacqueline Kennedy Garden	*Jardin (Jacqueline Kennedy) de*	*(Ost-) Garten*	*Jardín este*	*Hortus Orientalis*
Kids	*Enfants*	*Kinder*	*Niños*	*Liberi*
Kite!	*Cerf-volant!*	*Drachen!*	*¡Barrilete!*	*Milvus!*

FIRST LADY JACQUELINE KENNEDY

PRESIDENT JOHN F. KENNEDY

CAROLINE KENNEDY   JOHN F. KENNEDY JR.

L

A B C D E F G H I J K · M N O P Q R S T U V W X Y Z

l

Abraham Lincoln	*Abraham Lincoln*	*Abraham Lincoln*	*Abrahán Lincoln*	*Pater Multorum Lindum*
Library	*Bibliothèque*	*Bibliothek*	*Biblioteca*	*Bibliotheca*
Lamp	*Lampe*	*Lampe*	*Lámpara*	*Lucerna*
Light	*Lumière*	*Licht*	*Luz*	*Lux*
Leader!	*Chef!*	*Leiter!*	*¡Líder!*	*Dux!*

BENJAMIN LATROBE

PRESIDENT ABRAHAM LINCOLN

MONCHOUSIA

M
A B C D E F G H I J K L · N O P Q R S T U V W X Y Z
m

James Madison	*Jacques Madison*	*Jakob Madison*	*Jaime Madison*	*Iacobus Maudi*
James Monroe	*Jacques Monroe*	*Jakob Monroe*	*Jaime Monroe*	*Iacobus Monrovius*
William McKinley	*Guillaume McKinley*	*Wilhelm McKinley*	*Guillermo McKinley*	*Gulielmus Cinlei*
Map Room	*Salle des Cartes*	*Kartenzimmer*	*Salón de los Mapas*	*Conclave Tabularum*
Muffin	*Muffin*	*Törtchen*	*Panecillo*	*Panis*
Marvelous!	*Merveilleux!*	*Herrlich!*	*¡Maravilloso!*	*Mirabilis!*

PRESIDENT WILLIAM MCKINLEY

PRESIDENT JAMES MONROE

PRESIDENT JAMES MADISON   FIRST LADY DOLLEY MADISON

Richard M. Nixon	*Richard M. Nixon*	*Richard M. Nixon*	*Ricardo M. Nixon*	*Ricardus Nicholi*
North Portico	*Portique Nord*	*Nördlicher Portikus*	*Pórtico Norte*	*Porticus Septentrionalis*
Nation	*Nation*	*Nation*	*Nación*	*Patria*
Newspaper	*Journal*	*Zeitung*	*Periódico*	*Acta publica*
Noble edifice!	*Édifice majestueux!*	*Nobeles Gebäude!*	*¡Noble edificio!*	*Aedificium Decorum!*

PRESIDENT RICHARD M. NIXON

North Portico

Oval Office	*Bureau ovale*	*Das ovale Büro*	*Oficina ovalada*	*Ovata Officina*
Offspring	*Enfant*	*Nachwuchs*	*Descendencia*	*Natus*
Open	*Ouvert(e)*	*Offen*	*Abierto*	*Apertus*
O.K.!	*D`accord!*	*O.K.!*	*¡Está bien!*	*Bene!*

PRESIDENT JOHN F. KENNEDY   JOHN F. KENNEDY JR.

PRESIDENT FRANKLIN PIERCE

PRESIDENT JAMES K. POLK

P

A B C D E F G H I J K L M N O · Q R S T U V W X Y Z

p

James K. Polk	*Jacques K. Polk*	*Jakob K. Polk*	*Jaime K. Polk*	*Iacobus Pelagius*
Franklin Pierce	*Franklin Pierce*	*Franklin Pierce*	*Franklin Pierce*	*Franciscus Petrus*
Pets	*Animaux domestiques*	*Haustiere*	*Mascotas*	*Animalia*
Police	*Police*	*Polizei*	*Policía*	*Lictores*
Parade!	*Défilé!*	*Umzug!*	*¡Desfile!*	*Pompa!*

PETALESHARRO

Pets on Parade

Queens' Bedroom	*Chambre de la Reine*	*Schlafzimmer der Königin*	*Dormitorio de la Reina*	*Cubiculum Reginae*
Quilt	*Édredon*	*Steppdecke*	*Edredón*	*Lodix Reticulata*
Quill	*Plume*	*Federkiel*	*Plumas de ave*	*Penna*
Quiet, please!	*Silence, s'il vous plaît!*	*Bitte Ruhe!*	*¡Silencio por favor!*	*Quiesce, amabo te!*

QUENTIN ROOSEVELT

QUEENS' BEDROOM

PRESIDENT RONALD REAGAN

R
A B C D E F G H I J K L M N O P Q · S T U V W X Y Z
r

Theodore Roosevelt	*Théodore Roosevelt*	*Theodor Roosevelt*	*Teodoro Roosevelt*	*Theodorus Agerrosarum*
Franklin D. Roosevelt	*Franklin D. Roosevelt*	*Franklin D. Roosevelt*	*Franklin D. Roosevelt*	*Franciscus Agerrosarum*
Ronald Reagan	*Ronald Reagan*	*Ronald Reagan*	*Renaldo Reagan*	*Ronaldus Regulus*
Rose Garden	*Jardin des Roses*	*Rosengarten*	*Jardín de las Rosas*	*Hortus Rosarum*
Rough Rider	*Cavalier intrépide*	*Verwegener Reiter*	*Soldado de caballería*	*Eques Durus*
Rambunctious!	*Tapageur!*	*Ungestüm!*	*¡Revoltoso!*	*Impiger!*

FIRST LADY ELEANOR ROOSEVELT

PRESIDENT FRANKLIN D. ROOSEVELT

PRESIDENT THEODORE ROOSEVELT

WILL ROGERS

A B C D E F G H I J K L M N O P Q R · T U V W X Y Z

S

s

State Dining Room	*Salle à Manger Officielle*	*Offizielles Esszimmer*	*Comedor del Estado*	*Cenaculum Civitatis*
Seventh President	*Septième président*	*Der siebente Präsident*	*Séptimo presidente*	*Septimus Praefectus*
Senator	*Sénateur*	*Senator*	*Senador*	*Senator*
Silver	*Argent*	*Silber*	*Vajilla de plata*	*Argentum*
Splendid!	*Splendide!*	*Hervorragend!*	*¡Espléndida!*	*Luculentus!*

JOHN PHILIP SOUSA

DOLPHIN LEG SOFA

PRESIDENT ANDREW JACKSON   SENATOR THOMAS HART BENTON

John Tyler	*Jean Tyler*	*Johann Tyler*	*Juan Tyler*	*Ioannes Tegulator*
Zachary Taylor	*Zacharie Taylor*	*Zacharias Taylor*	*Zacarías Taylor*	*Zechariah Textor*
William H. Taft	*Guillaume H. Taft*	*Wilhelm H. Taft*	*Guillermo H. Taft*	*Gulielmus H. Taft*
Harry S. Truman	*Harry S. Truman*	*Harry S. Truman*	*Harry S. Truman*	*Henricus Verivir*
West Terrace	*Terrace Ouest*	*West-Terrasse*	*Patio Oeste*	*Occidua Area*
Tea	*Thé*	*Tee*	*Té*	*Frondosa Potio*
Tasty!	*Délicieux!*	*Köstlich!*	*¡Sabroso!*	*Bene Gustatum!*

SOJOURNER TRUTH

THE PRESIDENT'S OWN

PRESIDENT JOHN TYLER   PRESIDENT ZACHARY TAYLOR

         PRESIDENT WILLIAM. H. TAFT   PRESIDENT HARRY S. TRUMAN

United States	*États-Unis*	*Vereinigte Staaten*	*Estados Unidos*	*Civitates Foederatae*
Uncle Sam	*Oncle Sam*	*Onkel Sam*	*Tío Sam*	*Patruus Samuelis*
Unusually	*Exceptionnellement*	*Ungewöhnlich*	*Tetera*	*Praeter consuetudinem*
Useful	*Utile*	*Nützlich*	*Insólitamente*	*Utilis*
Urn!	*Urne!*	*Urne!*	*¡Útil!*	*Urna!*

Uncle Sam

V
A B C D E F G H I J K L M N O P Q R S T U · W X Y Z
v

Martin Van Buren	*Martin Van Buren*	*Martin Van Buren*	*Martín Van Buren*	*Martinus Bureni*
Vermeil Room	*Salon de vermeil*	*Vergoldet Zimmer*	*Salón dorado*	*Cella aurea*
Vivacious	*Enjoué*	*Lebhaft*	*Animado*	*Alacris*
Very valuable!	*Très précieux!*	*Sehr wertvoll!*	*¡Muy valioso!*	*Pretiosissima!*

Angelica Van Buren   President Martin Van Buren

George Washington	*Georges Washington*	*Georg Washington*	*Jorge Washington*	*Georgius Vasintonianus*
Woodrow Wilson	*Woodrow Wilson*	*Woodrow Wilson*	*Woodrow Wilson*	*Vodrovius Gulielmi*
White House	*Maison Blanche*	*Das Weiße Haus*	*Casa Blanca*	*Domus Alba*
Wallpaper?	*Tapisserie?*	*Tapete?*	*¿Empapelado?*	*Charta muri?*
Wonderful!	*Merveilleux!*	*Wunderbar!*	*¡Maravilloso!*	*Mirabilis!*

PRESIDENT WOODROW WILSON

BOOKER T. WASHINGTON

PRESIDENT GEORGE WASHINGTON

FIRST LADY MARTHA WASHINGTON

Japanese Threadleaf Maple

Horse Chestnut   American Cork Tree

A B C D E F G H I J K L M N O P Q R S T U V W X · Z

Y
y

Yellow Oval Room	*Salon ovale jaune*	*Das gelbe ovale Zimmer*	*Salón ovalado amarillo*	*Croceum Ovatum Conclave*
Yes?	*Oui?*	*Ja?*	*¿Sí?*	*Sic?*
You are too young!	*Tu es trop!*	*Du auch*	*¡Eres tan Joven!*	*Adulescens Es!*

YO-YO MA

FIRST LADY JULIA GRANT   JESSE GRANT

Zealous	*Dévoué*	*Fleißig*	*Entusiasta*	*Ardens*
Zouave	*Zouave*	*Zuave*	*Guardia*	*Zoava*
Zebra	*Zèbre*	*Zebra*	*Cebra*	*Virgatus Equus*
Zoo!	*Zoo!*	*Zoo!*	*¡Zoológico!*	*Horti Animalium!*

ELMER ELLSWORTH

HISTORICAL NOTES

Unless otherwise noted, all items are drawn from the White House Collection, and all views of the White House are contemporary and modeled on the appearance of the house between 1996 and 2000.

FRONTISPIECE
George Washington teaches us the Presidential ABCs! He stands in front of the richly decorated north entrance to the White House. Its roses, leaves, acorns, griffins, ribbons, and bows were carved by Scottish stonemasons. President Washington's blackboard was modeled on the neoclassical furniture seen in his 1797 portrait by Gilbert Stuart, a painting still in the White House Collection.

COPYRIGHT PAGE
A sketch of the north facade of the White House, as seen from Pennsylvania Avenue. The tiny figure at right is Benjamin Latrobe, one of the architects who helped design the building.

DEDICATION PAGE
Dolley Madison flees from a group of British soldiers. She is holding the 1797 Gilbert Stuart portrait of Washington that she saved from the burning of the White House in 1814 and which remains in the White House Collection.

A
John Adams, the first president to live in the White House, arrives and is greeted by the original architect, James Hoban, in 1800. Artisans are still at work! The view of the north entrance of the White House follows Hoban's presentation drawing of 1793. The portrait of Hoban is based on an original miniature in wax. The cart brings household items, prominent among them a distinctive Sheffield coffee or tea urn (English, c. 1785–88) known to be one of Adams's "most prized possessions."

In the margin: President Chester A. Arthur, President John Quincy Adams, and First Lady Abigail Adams, wife of John Adams and mother of John Quincy Adams.

B
President James Buchanan greets President George Bush and his son President George W. Bush in the Blue Room. Historical details include a mantel clock depicting the Carthaginian general Hannibal (Paris, c. 1817), an enclosed armchair (bergère) by Bellangé (Paris, c. 1817), and a French center table (also c. 1817). All these items were purchased by President James Monroe.

In the margin: Members of the first Japanese delegation to the United States carry a *chigai-dana* lacquer cabinet (Japan, c. 1854), a gift to President Franklin Pierce. The delegation was received in the White House by President James Buchanan in 1860. A well-dressed American bison bows at top left.

C

In the China Room a cat examines presidential china. The pieces include a James Madison dessert cooler (on the table, Nast Manufactory, Paris, c. 1806); a John Quincy Adams salt cellar (on the floor, fourth from left, Meissen, Saxony, early 19th century); two Franklin Pierce pieces—a centerpiece and a compote (on the floor, far right and third from left, respectively, both Paris, decorated by Haughwout and Dailey, New York, 1853); a Ulysses S. Grant compote (on the floor, second from left, Haviland and Co., Limoges, 1869–70, 1874); a Rutherford B. Hayes coffee cup (on the floor, second from right, Haviland and Co., Limoges, c. 1880); a Benjamin Harrison coffee cup (on the table, Tressemannes and Vogt, Limoges, 1891); a tea and coffee set (on the floor under the chair, Lenox, Trenton, N.J., 1911) that belonged to William Howard Taft; a Harry S. Truman coffee cup (on the floor, far left, Lenox, Trenton, N.J., 1951). Also shown on the table is a Paul Storr candelabra (London, c. 1810–11). First Lady Grace Coolidge and her collie, Rob Roy, appear in a portrait in the background; the original is by Howard Chandler Christy, 1924.

Marching in the margin, from left to right: President William J. Clinton, President Jimmy Carter, President Calvin Coolidge, and President Grover Cleveland.

D

A dance at the White House, in the East Room as it was about 1866–67, during the Andrew Johnson administration. A bust of George Washington carved by Giuseppe Ceracchi in 1815 looks down on the proceedings from over the door. Refreshments are provided in a vermeil punch bowl made by George Wickes (London, c. 1739–40).

In the margin: Frederick Douglass, the abolitionist, who frequently visited the White House in the Lincoln and Andrew Johnson administrations. A dapper dog provides music for the festivities. A 19th-century donkey child runs to join his friends on the next page.

E

An Easter Egg Roll on the South Lawn, presided over by President Dwight D. Eisenhower The view of the South Portico shows the second story balcony still new in Eisenhower's time. It was added in 1948, during the Truman administration. The children are in late-19th-century costume. The tradition of the Easter Egg Roll on the White House grounds began in 1879, during the Hayes administration.

In the margin: An anonymous elephant child, also in 19th-century garb.

F

President Millard Fillmore and President Gerald R. Ford salute the American flag in front of the South Portico.

In the margin: First Lady Laura Bush reads to modern schoolchildren.

G

President James A. Garfield and President Ulysses S. Grant appear in a corner of the White House gardens. Grant is framed by a monumental gate or arch, formerly at the southeast corner of the President's Park, known from a water-color of c. 1820 by Anne-Marguerite Hyde de Neuville. The iron fence behind Garfield is adapted from an 1818 design by Paulus Hedl. Fences of this form were in use at the White House until 1902. Although almost hidden in the foliage, Garfield's seat is a cast-iron settee of an ornamental type still to be found in the gardens, possibly by Janes, Beebe of New York, c. 1852.

In the margin: A gopher with a geranium leaf.

H

Five presidents meet in the North Entrance Hall. President William Henry Harrison arrives on horseback. Shaking hands from left to right are President Rutherford B. Hayes, President Benjamin Harrison (the grandson of William Henry Harrison), President Herbert Hoover, and President Warren G. Harding.

In the margin: Presidential hats, including one of President Harry Truman's fedoras, President Abraham Lincoln's top hat, and President Theodore Roosevelt's Rough Rider hat.

I

Three presidents are shown in the rooms in which they were privately inaugurated at the White House. Each was subsequently publicly inaugurated at the U.S. Capitol. From left to right: Dwight D. Eisenhower in the East Room, with Chief Justice Earl Warren (January 20, 1957); Ronald Reagan in the Entrance Hall, with Chief Justice Warren Burger (January 20, 1985); Rutherford B. Hayes in the Red Room, with Chief Justice Morrison Waite (March 3, 1877). The figures in the crowd directly below each of the three ceremonies wear clothing of the appropriate period.

In the margin: A sprig of the ivy found in many places in the President's Park.

J

Thomas Jefferson is shown in his study in the southwest corner of the White House. He daydreams about the Lewis and Clark Expedition, which was sponsored by his administration, and is reading one of the journals of the expedition. Jefferson's study is reconstructed from written accounts. He was known to have had a long table with two drawers (containing gardening and carpenter's tools), haircloth-covered Windsor stools, maps, globes (one here has been marked with the Louisiana Purchase), and, of course, books in abundance. The windowsills are covered with samples of Jefferson's agricultural experiments. Magpies and prairie dogs were sent to the president by Lewis and Clark, among other flora and fauna, in 1805. The keelboat, or galley, on which Lewis, Clark, and Sacajawea, stand is based on one drawn in Lewis's journals. Jefferson is seated in a painted armchair (French, c. 1784–89) known to have belonged to him, and later to First Lady Dolley Madison.

Three other presidents are shown in the margin: President Andrew Johnson, President Lyndon B. Johnson, and President Andrew Jackson.

K

President John F. Kennedy and his children, Caroline and John Jr., fly kites in the East Garden (also known as the Jacqueline Kennedy Garden).

In the margin: First Lady Jacqueline Kennedy holds an enlarged copy of *The White House: An Historic Guide*, which, at her instigation, was first published in 1962.

L

President Abraham Lincoln writes letters by lamplight in the library. The mid-19th-century oil lamps that surround him are from the Lincoln Bedroom and the Lincoln Sitting Room. The brass inkwell is adapted from one in the Smithsonian Institution, thought likely to have been used by Lincoln in writing the Emancipation Proclamation. The rosewood armchair (American, c. 1861) in which he sits (only the top is visible) dates from the Lincoln presidency.

In the margin: A portrait of architect Benjamin Latrobe, the surveyor of public buildings appointed by Jefferson in 1803. He also designed furniture for the Madison White House.

M

President James Madison and First Lady Dolley Madison enjoy muffins in the Map Room. Historic decorative arts in the room include a cut-glass chandelier (English, c. 1771–73) and the armchair in which James Madison sits (attributed to Thomas Affleck, Philadelphia, c. 1765–75). Dolley Madison's wingback easy chair is attributed to Gilbert Ash (New York, c. 1760–80). The high chest of drawers at left was made in Philadelphia, c. 1770.

In the margin: President William McKinley and President James Monroe hold maps of the United States during their administrations. Also present is the Kansa chief, Monchousia. He was painted during the Monroe administration by Charles Bird King (c. 1821–22) at the time of his visit to the White House.

N

A view of the North Portico from the northeast. Members of the White House police in uniform are on guard in the corners.

In the margin: President Richard M. Nixon is reading a newspaper.

O

A view of the Oval Office, modeled on a famous photograph of President John F. Kennedy and his son, John F. Kennedy Jr. The focal point of the room is the Resolute Desk, the great white oak and mahogany desk (William Evenden, England, 1880) given to President Rutherford B. Hayes by Queen Victoria in 1880. The door in the front of the desk, from which John Jr. emerges, was added by President Franklin D. Roosevelt.

In the margin: An owl clutches the crystal newel post of the Grand Staircase.

P

A parade of White House pets, led by Quentin Roosevelt on his pony, Algonquin. He is aided by a White House police-man, c. 1900. President Theodore Roosevelt and First Lady Edith Roosevelt—father and mother of Quentin—look on in surprise from the South Portico. The pets represent several administrations in addition to that of Theodore Roosevelt: Fala the Dog (Franklin D. Roosevelt), Eli the Macaw (Theodore Roosevelt), His Whiskers the Goat (Benjamin Harrison), Rebecca the Raccoon (Grace Coolidge), Emily Spinach the Garter Snake (Theodore Roosevelt), Rex the Dog (Nancy Reagan), Socks the Cat (Bill Clinton), Josiah the Badger (Theodore Roosevelt), Bill the Horned Toad (Theodore Roosevelt), Jonathan Edward Bear (Theodore Roosevelt), Sheep (Woodrow Wilson), Peter the Bull Terrier (Theodore Roosevelt), Father Grady the Guinea Pig (Theodore Roosevelt), Manchu the Spaniel (Theodore Roosevelt and Alice Roosevelt), Laddie Boy the Airedale (Warren G. Harding).

In the margin: Bust portraits of President Franklin Pierce, President James K. Polk, and Petalesharro, a Pawnee chief who visited the White House during the Monroe administration. His portrait was painted in c. 1821–22 by Charles Bird King.

Q

An imaginary view of the Queens' Bedroom. A regal visitor sleeps quietly within. No queen has ever lived in the White House, but several have come to visit and stay in this room. Historical objects include an early-19th-century bed that was possibly owned by Andrew Jackson. The patchwork quilt on the bed was made from fragments saved from the upholstery of furniture in the Red, Green, and East Rooms, c. 1897–1901. The side table is attributed to Thomas Seymour (Boston, 1814), and the tambour desk behind the bed is by Thomas and/or John Seymour (Boston, c. 1795–1810). A portrait of Fanny Kemble, a well-known 19th-century actress, is adapted from the original by Thomas Sully, 1834. She looks down with a quizzical smile on her visitor.

In the margin: Quentin Roosevelt appears for a second time in the book. He is resting after the parade on the "P" page. Also in the margin is a black marble mantel clock (France, c. 1833). It shows the royal bedtime—quarter past 10!

R

President Theodore Roosevelt in the guise of a Rough Rider in the modern Rose (West) Garden. Several rabbits, helping the gardeners, are surprised to see him there!

In the margin: Portraits of President Ronald Reagan, First Lady Eleanor Roosevelt, and President Franklin D. Roosevelt. Also found: Will Rogers, entertainer and humorist, a famous visitor to the Franklin Roosevelt White House.

S

Andrew Jackson, the seventh president, hosts a dinner in the State Dining Room. The honored guest, at right, is Senator Thomas Hart Benton, a Jackson political ally. Much of the silver on the table is from a set purchased in 1833 during the Jackson administration (M.G. Biennais, Paris, c. 1809–19) and includes a mustard stand, cruet stand, cream jug, and vegetable dish. The wine cooler at left is from the Monroe administration (J.B.C. Odiot, Paris, 1798–1809).

In the margin: Another Biennais piece, a soup tureen from the same set noted above, and an Empire sofa (New York, c. 1810–25) from the Red Room. Also here: a portrait of John Philip Sousa, famous composer of marches and leader of the Marine Band, "the President's Own," from 1880 to 1892.

T

Four presidents are shown at a tea party on the West Terrace. President William Howard Taft, first president to hold social events on the White House terraces, acts as host to President John Tyler, President Zachary Taylor, and President Harry S. Truman. The teacups used were part of a set given to Taft on his 25th anniversary (Lenox, 1911).

In the margin: Sojourner Truth, the abolitionist, who is known to have met with President Abraham Lincoln in the White House. Also seen is a pardoned Thanksgiving turkey, at upper left. Several members of the Marine Band, "the President's Own," all playing instruments that start with a "T," march in the bottom margin behind their drum major.

U

Uncle Sam, the weather being unpleasant, has forsaken his umbrella for a cup of coffee. He pours out from a silver plate Sheffield coffee or tea urn (English, c. 1785–88) that belonged to John and Abigail Adams, portraits of whom look down approvingly from the walls. The mock bamboo side chair at left is from either the Grant or the Hayes administration (New York, c. 1873–77). Uncle Sam stands on an imaginary folk art hooked rug that features a map of the United States. At left stands an unusual hinged work table, attributed to Duncan Phyfe (c. 1810) and which customarily resides in the Green Room. On the table is a porcelain urn by Barr, Flight and Barr (Worcester, England, c. 1807).

In the margin: Another useful coffee urn. This one belonged to Millard Fillmore (Wood and Hughes, New York, c. 1858).

V

President Martin Van Buren and his daughter-in-law, Angelica Singleton Van Buren, toast each other in the Vermeil Room using goblets from the White House Collection. His goblet is by Joseph Jackson (Dublin, c. 1775–87); hers is by Tiffany and Co. (New York, c. 1937–47). Other items from the vermeil (gilded silver) collection are seen on the wall behind them: a wine cooler by Paul Storr (London, c. 1809–10), two ewers by Richard Sibley (London, c. 1817–18), and a punch bowl by George Wickes (London, c. 1739–40).

In the margin are more vermeil items: a covered jam pot by P.J.B. Huguet (Paris, c. 1806–16), a lion-footed salt cellar by Paul Storr (London, c. 1809–10), a wine cooler by Philip Rundell (London, 1823), and a Tiffany compote (New York, c. 1882).

W

President George Washington points to James Hoban's 1793 presentation drawing of the future White House. Although he never lived there, the design was approved by Washington. By implication, Washington also introduces the new institution of the American presidency, which he so strongly influenced. Small, framed portraits of Hoban and Benjamin Latrobe, the two major architects to work on the building in its early years, are hung above the drawing. Washington's pose is modeled, in reverse, on that seen in the majestic Gilbert Stuart portrait of 1797 in the White House Collection. The eagle on the wallpaper sample is inspired by that found on china owned by James Monroe, c. 1817.

In the margin: First Lady Martha Washington, seated, admires her husband's projects. President Woodrow Wilson holds a book; he was also the president of Princeton University. Booker T. Washington, another famous educator, stands nearby. He visited the White House during the Theodore Roosevelt administration.

X

A couple, a child, and a dog enjoy a walk among magnificent trees in the President's Park. These two pictures take as their subject three specific trees from the grounds. These are, from left to right, a large Japanese threadleaf maple planted in 1893 by First Lady Frances Cleveland, a horse chestnut, and an American cork tree. Xs are formed by the branches of these trees and some of the shadows they cast.

In the margin: Xs are also formed by the backs or bases of three chairs in the White House Collection. These are: a klismos chair designed by Latrobe, c. 1809 (destroyed in 1814; it makes one X); a Duncan Phyfe armchair (New York, c. 1810-20; it makes two); and a side chair attributed to the Samuel McIntire workshop (Salem, Mass., c. 1800; it makes four!).

Y

First Lady Julia Grant and her son Jesse talk in the Yellow Oval Room. Jesse seeks permission to play with a "yacht" (actually a silver centerpiece in the form of a "Hiawatha Boat," Gorham, Providence, R.I., 1871) that his mother had selected at the Centennial Exhibition in Philadelphia in 1876. The conference table (Pottier and Stymus, New York, 1869) is another historic piece from the Grant administration.

In the margin: Mrs. Grant's chair (Pottier and Stymus, New York, 1869), from which she has risen to discuss the matter of the yacht with Jesse, is left vacant. Yo-Yo Ma, the famous cellist, plays heavenly music "from above." He performed in the White House during the Clinton administration.

Z

The White House, as seen in a view based on an anonymous watercolor of c. 1825, rests peacefully under the watchful eye of Elmer Ellsworth. Ellsworth was the colonel of a Civil War–era Zouave regiment and a friend of Abraham Lincoln. Zouave regiments were organized by both sides during the Civil War. Their ornate costumes were modeled on those of the North African regiments of the French Army in this period, units admired for their bravery. In the middleground, a small, informal zoo has been arranged on the grounds, behind the bars of a zigzagging fence.

In the margin: Children in old and modern dress "zoom" toward the zoo.

PRESIDENTS OF THE UNITED STATES

1 *George Washington 1789–97*

2 *John Adams 1797–1801*

3 *Thomas Jefferson 1801–9*

4 *James Madison 1809–17*

5 *James Monroe 1817–25*

6 *John Quincy Adams 1825–29*

7 *Andrew Jackson 1829–37*

8 *Martin Van Buren 1837–41*

9 *William H. Harrison 1841*

10 *John Tyler 1841–45*

11 *James K. Polk 1845–49*

12 *Zachary Taylor 1849–50*

13 *Millard Fillmore 1850–53*

14 *Franklin Pierce 1853–57*

15 *James Buchanan 1857–61*

16 *Abraham Lincoln 1861–65*

17 *Andrew Johnson 1865–69*

18 *Ulysses S. Grant 1869–77*

19 *Rutherford B. Hayes 1877 81*

20 *James A. Garfield 1881*

21 *Chester A. Arthur 1881–85*

22 *Grover Cleveland 1885–89*

23 *Benjamin Harrison 1889–93*

24 *Grover Cleveland 1893–97*

25 *William McKinley 1897–1901*

26 *Theodore Roosevelt 1901–9*

27 *William H. Taft 1909–13*

28 *Woodrow Wilson 1913–21*

29 *Warren G. Harding 1921–23*

30 *Calvin Coolidge 1923–29*

31 *Herbert Hoover 1929–33*

32 *Franklin D. Roosevelt 1933–45*

33 *Harry S. Truman 1945–53*

34 *Dwight D. Eisenhower 1953–61*

35 *John F. Kennedy 1961–63*

36 *Lyndon B. Johnson 1963–69*

37 *Richard M. Nixon 1969–74*

38 *Gerald R. Ford 1974–77*

39 *Jimmy Carter 1977–81*

40 *Ronald Reagan 1981–89*

41 *George Bush 1989–93*

42 *William J. Clinton 1993–2001*

43 *George W. Bush 2001–*

JOHN HUTTON

THE WHITE HOUSE ABC
was set in Monotype Baskerville, a typeface
designed by John Baskerville in 1750.

DESIGN AND TYPOGRAPHY BY THORNWILLOW PRESS, LTD.

NEW YORK · WEST STOCKBRIDGE · PRAGUE

"ARS OMNIA TUETUR"